CAMBRIDGE LIBRARY COLLECTION

Books of enduring scholarly value

Literary Studies

This series provides a high-quality selection of early printings of literary works, textual editions, anthologies and literary criticism which are of lasting scholarly interest. Ranging from Old English to Shakespeare to early twentieth-century work from around the world, these books offer a valuable resource for scholars in reception history, textual editing, and literary studies.

The Cambridge Reinaert Fragments

The Reinaert Fragments are a collection of seven pages of a Middle Dutch poem attributed to the fifteenth-century Flemish writer Hinrek van Alckmer, and printed in Antwerp in about 1487. This book, originally published in 1927, contains photographic reproductions of the pages, alongside clear transcriptions of the text and three beautiful woodcut illustrations. Karl Breul's detailed introduction sketches the history and development of the story of Reynard the Fox, from its origins in oral tradition and the medieval beast epic to Goethe's famous 'Reinecke Fuchs', indicating the place of the Reinaert poem amongst the various verse and prose versions. The book also includes a corrected version of the van Alckmer fragments, and examines their relationship with the Reinaert II and Reinke texts. The book will be useful to those studying Middle Dutch and Middle Low German literature or printing history, and others interested in the Reynard story.

T0371568

Cambridge University Press has long been a pioneer in the reissuing of out-of-print titles from its own backlist, producing digital reprints of books that are still sought after by scholars and students but could not be reprinted economically using traditional technology. The Cambridge Library Collection extends this activity to a wider range of books which are still of importance to researchers and professionals, either for the source material they contain, or as landmarks in the history of their academic discipline.

Drawing from the world-renowned collections in the Cambridge University Library, and guided by the advice of experts in each subject area, Cambridge University Press is using state-of-the-art scanning machines in its own Printing House to capture the content of each book selected for inclusion. The files are processed to give a consistently clear, crisp image, and the books finished to the high quality standard for which the Press is recognised around the world. The latest print-on-demand technology ensures that the books will remain available indefinitely, and that orders for single or multiple copies can quickly be supplied.

The Cambridge Library Collection will bring back to life books of enduring scholarly value (including out-of-copyright works originally issued by other publishers) across a wide range of disciplines in the humanities and social sciences and in science and technology.

The Cambridge Reinaert Fragments

(Culemann Fragments)

EDITED BY KARL BREUL

CAMBRIDGE
UNIVERSITY PRESS

CAMBRIDGE UNIVERSITY PRESS

Cambridge, New York, Melbourne, Madrid, Cape Town, Singapore,
São Paolo, Delhi, Dubai, Tokyo, Mexico City

Published in the United States of America by Cambridge University Press, New York

www.cambridge.org
Information on this title: www.cambridge.org/9781108010153

© in this compilation Cambridge University Press 2010

This edition first published 1927
This digitally printed version 2010

ISBN 978-1-108-01015-3 Paperback

The Cambridge Reinaert Fragments

CAMBRIDGE
UNIVERSITY PRESS
LONDON : Fetter Lane

NEW YORK
The Macmillan Co.
BOMBAY, CALCUTTA and
MADRAS
Macmillan and Co., Ltd.
TORONTO
The Macmillan Co. of
Canada, Ltd.
TOKYO
Maruzen-Kabushiki-Kaisha

The Cambridge Reinaert Fragments

(CULEMANN FRAGMENTS)

EDITED
WITH AN INTRODUCTION
& BIBLIOGRAPHY
BY

KARL BREUL, M.A., Litt.D., Ph.D.

SCHRÖDER PROFESSOR OF GERMAN IN THE
UNIVERSITY OF CAMBRIDGE

CAMBRIDGE
at the University Press
1927

Edition limited to 300 *copies*

.

PRINTED IN GREAT BRITAIN

TO

The Memory of

F. G. H. CULEMANN

AND

HENRY BRADSHAW

PREFACE

THE purpose of the present book is to make the unique 'Culemann Fragments' (preserved for more than half a century among the treasures of our University Library) accessible to students of Old Netherlandish and Old German literature by an exact photographic reproduction of the seven precious leaves. A brief account of the rise and development of the Medieval Beast Epic has been added in order to indicate the place they hold among the various verse and prose versions of the Reinaert story. The juxtaposition of the Netherlandish and the Lübeck texts makes it evident that Hinrek van Alckmer's 'Reinaert' is the immediate source of the famous Low German 'Reinke de Vos' from which nearly all subsequent versions are either translated or adapted.

It is not my present purpose to give a full account of the Medieval *Tiersage* and *Tierepos* in the Netherlands, France and Germany. This has been done adequately by other scholars, especially recently by Karl Voretzsch, but the selected Bibliography at the end of my brief Introduction will, together with the Table, be of use to readers who wish to make a more detailed study of the origins and literary development of the Medieval Beast Epic. It refers them to the more important books and articles dealing with various aspects of this fascinating subject. Some of the latest works mentioned in it contain further bibliographical references.

My own interest in the Fragments dates a long way back. My attention was first called to them by my revered teacher and friend, Professor Wilhelm Scherer of Berlin, and in 1883 I was privileged to discuss them in Hanover with Senator F. G. H. Culemann, the scholar by whom the leaves were discovered and after whom they were named.

vij

In 1887 I examined them closely in our University Library and wrote a short article (published in 1888 in Vol. xiv of Paul and Braune's 'Beiträge') in which I was able to make a few additions and corrections to the text of the Flemish fragments as published by Dr Friedrich Prien in his excellent edition of 'Reinke de vos' (1887) and in his valuable article on the previous history of Reinke (printed in Paul and Braune's 'Beiträge,' viii (1882), 10–16).

I wish to thank Mr A. F. Scholfield, M.A., Librarian of the Cambridge University Library, for his kindness in placing the dossier of the Culemann Fragments [Adv. 583] at my disposal and for allowing me to have the leaves photographed. The photographs were taken by Mr W. Tams with his usual success. I also wish to thank the Syndics of the University Press for their readiness to undertake the publication of this book, their Secretary, Mr S. C. Roberts, for the interest he has taken in it, and Miss M. Steele Smith, Tutor and Lecturer in English at Newnham College, for useful suggestions in preparing the manuscript for the Press.

K. B.

BARTON COTTAGE
  CAMBRIDGE

Christmas, 1926

TABLE OF CONTENTS

INTRODUCTION

A brief sketch of the origin and development of the Medieval Beast Epic in order to indicate the place of the Cambridge 'Reinaert' Fragments (the 'Culemann Fragments') among the Epics on Reynard the Fox.

THE genuine Beast Epic—as distinguished from short stories, fables with a didactic purpose, and the early short allegorical 'Physiologus' or 'Bestiary' stories—is not found in classical literature, but was the product of the Middle Ages, from the middle of the tenth to the end of the fifteenth centuries. The oldest versions were in Latin, written by monks who were evidently acquainted with popular traditions concerning the nature and doings of animals, and also well versed in classical Latin literature. The home of the early Beast Epic is Belgium, Lorraine and the North of France.

Apart from a number of minor poems, the first production of any length and unity is the *Ecbasis Captivi*, written about 940 in hexameters by a monk of German about 940 descent in the monastery St. Aper at Toul in Lorraine. The hero of the satirical poem is a calf which runs away from its stable but afterwards returns to it, *i.e.* a monk who leaves and subsequently returns to his monastery. The fox—still nameless—appears in part of the poem as an old enemy of the wolf, but he is not yet the hero.

YSENGRIMUS.

Nearly two centuries later we find another Latin poem, of much greater im- 1150-1152 portance, the so-called 'Ysengrimus.' It is a true epic, a remarkable production, written on Flemish soil, by the Magister Nivardus of Ghent. This clever poem is a production of considerable length, consisting of no less than 3287 distichs (6574 lines), and is divided into seven books. Although it contains a great number of classical allusions and reminiscences, it is largely based on oral tradition and popular stories. In this poem the animals are introduced for the first time by characteristic proper names which had obviously been coined in Flemish surroundings. This poem, now called 'Ysengrimus' (as edited by Voigt)[1], was called by

---

[1] See the Bibliography on p. xxiii under 3, and compare Karl Voretzsch, 'Einführung in das Studium der altfranzösischen Literatur.' Halle (Saale), [3]1925, p. 381.

former editors (Mone, J. Grimm) 'Reinardus Vulpes,' while Grimm's 'Ysengrimus is more properly styled 'Ysengrimus Abbreviatus.' 'Ysengrimus' is the first Beast Epic of importance in medieval literature.

REINHART FUCHS.

1182   About a generation later than 'Ysengrimus' appeared 'Reinhart Fuchs' (1182)[1] which is the oldest Medieval Beast Epic written in a popular language. It is 60 to 70 years older than the oldest Flemish 'Reinaert' and was produced on German soil in German by the Alsatian poet Heinrich der Glichezare. The original poem is preserved only in fragments, but a later remodelled version, perhaps made in the southern part of Bohemia, has come down to us in its entirety.

This Middle High German 'Reinhart Fuchs' is an artistic production compiled by a gifted poet from several 'branches'—no longer extant—of the Old French cycle called 'Roman de Renart.' The Alsatian poet combined these 'branches' skilfully in his continuous narrative to which he gave an artistic tragic ending.

The German poem thus represents an older stage of the 'Roman de Renart' than the one preserved in the numerous 'branches' that have come down to us. Although this South German Epic is a poem of real merit, it did not achieve the literary success of the Low German 'Reinke de Vos' which appeared more than 300 years later. This is no doubt partly due to the then recent invention of printing by means of which the younger 'Reinke' could be made known much more widely than the work of Heinrich der Glichezare of which only very few manuscripts were in existence.

after 1160   ## ROMAN DE RENART.

By the name 'Roman de Renart' is understood[2] not one complete and homogeneous epic poem, but a cycle consisting of a large number of so-called 'branches' of varying age and value, written by different poets. They made use of stories and traditions very similar to those utilised by the Magister Nivardus of Ghent. The home of the authors of these 'branches' was clearly the North of France,

[1] See Karl Voretzsch, 'Einf. i. d. Stud. d. afrz. Lit.' p. 382, and also his valuable Introduction to G. Baesecke's edition of 'Reinhart Fuchs' (1925). He is now engaged on a thorough investigation of the interrelation of 'Ysengrimus,' 'Reinhart' and the 'Roman de Renart.'

[2] See Karl Voretzsch, 'Einführung i. d. Stud. d. afrz. Lit.' pp. 374 sqq., where other references are given.

not far from the Flemish boundaries. Most of the writers were natives of Picardy, others lived in Normandy, the Île de France and Champagne.

The French 'branches' are unequal in value and were never welded by a gifted poet into a work of art, comparable to either the Latin 'Ysengrimus,' or the Alsatian 'Reinhart,' or the Flemish 'Reinaert' (I). These 'branches' as we know them now are all younger than the 'Ysengrimus.' Yet at the time there seem to have existed certain 'branches,' now lost, possibly composed not much later than the middle of the twelfth century (from about 1160 onwards). Their nature may be inferred from the Alsatian 'Reinhart Fuchs.' These older 'branches' were subsequently modified by younger minstrels.

Among the many French 'branches,' the 'branches' 1 (in older books called No. 20), 10, and 6, became of importance for the later development of the Netherlandish 'Reinaert' epics across the frontier on Flemish soil.

THE FLEMISH 'REINAERT' POEMS[1].

A. REINAERT I.

between
1235–1250

This, the older of the two Flemish versions of the 'Reinaert' epic in the thirteenth century, is written in short riming couplets and follows on the whole branch 1 of the 'Roman de Renart.' In the place-names it bears distinct traces of Flemish origin, and the names of the animals are mainly Flemish.

The poem consists of an older and a younger portion; the first is largely based on the French original, the younger portion contains a considerable amount of original work. The epic was produced by two poets, Willem and Aernout, but it is not absolutely certain which of them wrote the earlier and which the later portion. Both were gifted poets, and 'Reinaert I' is a true work of art. It was translated at an early date (1267–1273?) into Latin by the monk Balduinus, and it corresponds roughly to the first of the four books of the Low German 'Reinke de Vos.'

B. REINAERT II, REINAERTS HISTORIE.

about 1375

Some hundred years later (about 1375) the older 'Reinaert' (I) was remodelled and continued by another Flemish poet whose name we do not know. He called

---

[1] See the Bibliography on p. xxiii, under 7–10.

his work 'Reinaerts Historie.' This new poem, composed in the same metre as the older 'Reinaert,' was enlarged to 7794 lines. Its author took much of his new material from the sixth branch of the 'Roman de Renart' and also drew upon other branches. It is an interesting compilation and not without merit, although on the whole artistically inferior to 'Reinaert' (I). Much of it was borrowed from a variety of other literary sources, and the poet who has a decided satirical and didactic tendency makes the animals appear very human.

This 'Reinaert II' ('Reinaerts Historie'), including, as it does, in its first part a slightly modified version of 'Reinaert I,' was of the very greatest importance for the future development of the Beast Epic on Netherlandish and German soil. It was in *this* form that the Beast Epic came down to modern times. 'Reinaerts Historie' of the fourteenth century is found only in manuscript form.

On 'Reinaerts Historie' was based the first printed prose version, the oldest one 1479–1485 being printed at Gouda (1479) while another one was published soon after at Delft (1485). In these early printed versions there is still no division into (4) books. The Gouda book from which Caxton made the first English translation (in 1481) keeps very close to the old poetic version, the rimes of which are distinctly noticeable in many passages of the prose text. On the Delft version see Fr. Prien in P.B.B. VIII, 22 note. From these books sprang the widely read old chap-book 1564 (Antwerp, 1564) which was for a long time the only form in which the Netherlandish 'Reinaert' was known to the world. The subject-matter was the same as that contained in the Low German 'Reinke de Vos,' but it is clear that 'Reinke' was not derived from the prose book.

about 1480   C. THE 'CULEMANN FRAGMENTS.'

About 100 years after the composition of 'Reinaerts Historie' another Flemish writer, Hinrek van Alckmer, produced the first *printed* poetic 'Reinaert' (II) and added a moralising gloss to the slightly revised poem. About the personality of Hinrek, the author of the early printed book now represented only by the few fragments (F.) preserved in Cambridge University Library, there has been much discussion[1]. It would be interesting if Professor Muller, or some other Dutch or Belgian scholar, would investigate the matter still further.

[1] Especially by Friedrich Prien (in P.B.B. VIII, 2 sqq., and in his edition of 'Reinke de vos' (1887), xiii–xiv and 274), and by Professor J. W. Muller, of Leiden, in various places (quoted in Prien's and in Leitzmann's editions. See p. xxiv).

The 'Culemann Fragments' (F.)[1] are a very small portion of Hinrek van Alckmer's first printed edition. His work represents the latest stage of the 'Reinaert' poem in which the text was probably for the first time divided into four books, each of them being again subdivided into a number of chapters. To the verse narrative were prefixed short prose summaries of the contents. In this edition there were also added for the first time a large number of excellent wood-cuts of which three have been preserved in F. As stated above, the learned author introduced after the illustrations and before the poetic text of each chapter moralising glosses in prose of which but little has escaped the scissors of the binders who cut down the leaves of the book from which F. were taken. Hinrek van Alckmer would appear to have kept closely to the text of 'Reinaerts Historie' with slight alterations and additions of his own. The existence of this most important printed poetic version was altogether unknown till 1854 when Senator F. G. H. Culemann made his important find[2].

REINKE DE VOS.

This is the title of the famous late Middle Low German poem which first appeared at Lübeck in 1498 and was probably printed by Matthaeus Brandis. It had long been realised that the 'Reinke' was dependent on 'Reinaert II,' but it contained a prose gloss and was divided into books and chapters that were absent from 'Reinaerts Historie' as it was then known. It seemed probable that there must have existed a text between 'Reinke' and the manuscripts of 'Reinaert II' of which the former was a translation. This long-suspected missing link, by which also the Flemish prose chap-book (Antwerp, 1564) was influenced, was supplied by the lucky discovery of the 'Culemann Fragments[3].' From them it is now evident that the Low German author of R.V. is not—as had long been thought —an original poet, but rather a not unskilful translator. It is, however, not to be wondered at that for many centuries the author of R.V. was considered an original poet of great merit because the Netherlandish original had practically vanished, the manuscripts of 'Reinaert' were unknown and unpublished, the old printed editions had been destroyed by the zeal of the clergy[4]. The translation

[1] For details see pp. 2–27.   [2] See pp. xvii sqq.
[3] See the parallel texts on pp. 30–49 of this edition.
[4] They were placed for instance on the Index librorum prohibitorum of the University of Louvain (in 1550).

of the Flemish poem into Low German did not for the most part present any great difficulties, as the dialects were still very similar and many of the Netherlandish rimes could be reproduced exactly in the Low German poem. The gloss in R.V. is considerably longer and much freer than the gloss found in F., but apparently the idea of adding prose moralisations was suggested to the author of R.V. by the glosses he met with in F. The gloss in R.V. was originally a Roman Catholic gloss. Subsequently a Protestant gloss (by Ludwig Dietz?) was added to the text of the poem. It appears for the first time in the Rostock edition of 1539.

The Low German 'Reinke de Vos' was translated into High German and into many other languages[1]. The first High German translation was published at Frankfort on the Main in 1544. Most of the translations were adorned by numerous wood-cuts. As early as 1567 A. Schopper's able rendering into Latin iambics was published at Frankfort. Gottsched's widely read High German prose version (to which the Low German text was added in an appendix) came out in 1752, and Goethe's ingenious 'Reinecke Fuchs' (1794), in hexameter verse, which delighted the Germans in a time of great political and social ferment, was largely based on this. Goethe's epic, in 12 cantos containing 4312 hexameters, was undertaken primarily to obtain practice in the handling of the Homeric metre and was written in three months (January to March 1793). It was first published early in 1794. Goethe kept on the whole very close to Gottsched's prose paraphrase but no doubt referred occasionally to the Low German original given at the end of Gottsched's edition. He comes often wonderfully near to 'Reinke' and to 'Reinaert.' In Goethe's poem parts of Cantos III and IV correspond to the Culemann Fragments, viz. Canto III, lines 280 to end, and Canto IV, lines 1–90[2].

Goethe's 'Reinecke Fuchs' was published in a large 4º edition, with many most successful illustrations by Wilhelm von Kaulbach, at Stuttgart and Tübingen, Cotta, 1846. In some of Kaulbach's pictures the same scenes are illustrated as in the 'Culemann Fragments.' On page 52 of the Kaulbach edition we see the fox running away with the capon, the priest upsetting the table; and on p. 58 the fox is running after chickens.

---

[1] See F. Prien's valuable bibliography on pp. xxxviii–lxxiv of his edition.
[2] See Goethes Werke VI (Cotta Jubilee edition), pp. 31 sqq.

In Gottsched's edition a number of fine etchings by Allart van Everdingen were included. Goethe admired them very much and purchased a set in 1783.

THE CULEMANN FRAGMENTS[1].

The so-called 'Culemann Fragments' consist of seven leaves in small 4° of the same size as the exact reproductions given in this book. Two of them are well pre-served, one fairly so, while four are more or less mutilated[2]. Their value and place in literary history were discovered, in 1854, by Senator F. G. H. Culemann of Hanover, who bought them in the early fifties of last century from Edwin Tross, a Parisian bookseller. Tross had discovered and removed the seven leaves from an old Dutch printed book, the title and contents of which are unknown. The Fragments (F.) were acquired in February 1870 for the Cambridge University Library by its Librarian Henry Bradshaw from a sale of the Culemann Collection by B. Quaritch in London. They are now preserved, together with Culemann's unique reprint, a few notes, three letters, and some printed matter referring to them, under 'Adv. 583' in the University Library. The first account of Culemann's find was given by Karl Gödeke, in his 'Deutsche Wochenschrift,' 1854, Heft 8, p. 256; it was soon followed by Hoffmann von Fallersleben's notice in 'Algemeene Konst- en Letterbode,' 1855, No. 36. Culemann never published an account of the Fragments himself but only printed the greater part of them privately under the title 'Brokken eens ouden druks van den Reinaert in verzen.' The only copy of this reprint[3], very probably only proof-sheets, is preserved at Cambridge together with the original leaves which have been carefully repaired and bound.

[1] An accurate description and full discussion of them were first given by Friedrich Prien in Paul and Braune's 'Beiträge zur Geschichte der deutschen Sprache und Literatur,' VIII (1882), pp. 8–21, on which was based the brief account in the Introduction to his valuable edition of 'Reinke de vos' (Halle, 1887), pp. xii–xiv. See also Karl Breul in P.B.B. XIV (1888), pp. 377–8, and Karl Voretzsch in Albert Leitzmann's edition of 'Reinke de vos' (Halle, 1925), pp. xxvi–xxvii, largely based on Prien's previous edition. Prien's account of the Cambridge Reinaert Fragments in P.B.B. VIII was based on very full information received in 1879 and 1880 from Mr G. A. S. Schneider, B.A. (now the Rev. G. A. S. Schneider, M.A., Librarian of Gonville and Caius College, Cambridge), and, through Mr Schneider, from Henry Brad-shaw, University Librarian, a great authority on early printed books. See also pp. xx–xxi.

[2] See Prien's Introduction to his edition, pp. xii–xiii.

[3] See p. xx, under 1.

The three letters which need not be printed here were written to Culemann by Friedrich Zarncke (2) and by Karl Gödeke (1). In Zarncke's first letter (dated 26 January 1854) he congratulates Culemann on his find, urges a speedy publication and says that he would be glad to be of assistance. Culemann replied to this on the 28th (note on top of the letter: pr. 27 Jan., resp. 28 Jan.). Gödeke wrote to Culemann on the 29th of January suggesting Zarncke as a possible editor of the Fragments, and in the 'Deutsche Wochenschrift' he had already announced 'Die Veröffentlichung des Fundes wird Herr Dr Fr. Zarncke in Leipzig besorgen.' Zarncke, however, in the second letter (of 23 April 1854) to Culemann regrets 'Gödekes naseweise Übereilung,' states that he will not edit the Fragments but asks for a statement that he had refused the editorship owing to pressure of work. Hoffmann von Fallersleben, the first editor, does not mention this episode in his short Preface[1].

The seven leaves of the Fragments are part of the first book of an illustrated and glossed Reinaert in four books, printed, probably in 1487, at Antwerp by Ger. Leeu[2].

The Text. Of the Reinaert II text represented by F. 196 lines are well preserved, 27 (*i.e.* 3 and 24) mutilated, and 16 entirely cut away. Only part of the contents of four chapters are preserved in F., viz. 90 lines (1–90) of Chapter XVII (?), 20 lines (90–110) of Chapter XIX (?), 50 lines (111–161) of Chapter XXII, and 64 lines (162–225, of which 27 are partially cut away) of Chapter XXIII[3].

Headings of Chapters. Of these three (XXII, XXIII, XXIV) are complete, one (XIX?) is incomplete, one (XVII?) is missing altogether. After the heading of Chapter XXIV no illustration, gloss or verses follow. In three cases the headings of F. and of 'Reinke de Vos' (R.V.) either agree or are very similar. It is therefore most likely—although, owing to the scanty material, it cannot be proved with absolute certainty—that the author of R.V. made use of the headings of F. If he did not, he can only have used a slightly later and different version of F. now entirely lost to us. But this is very improbable[4].

The Gloss. The same holds good of the gloss[5]. The author of the moralising

---

[1] See p. xxiii, under 10.

[2] This was Bradshaw's view, in a MS. note of his among the papers kept in the dossier 'Adv. 583' in the University Library; see also P.B.B. VIII, 9.

[3] See P.B.B. VIII, 30–32. [4] See also P.B.B. VIII, 34.

[5] See P.B.B. VIII, 40.

prose comment on the chapters in verse is Hinrek van Alckmer. Only a few lines of one gloss quite at the beginning have been preserved. They differ considerably from the long moralisation that is placed *after* the text in R.V. (Prien's ed. pp. 62–63), while the gloss in F. is much shorter and is placed *before* the poetic text. Only a few words remain of a second gloss (see p. 23 top).

Wood-cuts. Two of the three attractive wood-cuts in F. occur also in R.V.; the illustrations in the Lübeck 'Reinke' are clearly reproductions of the Netherlandish illustrations, probably of those actually preserved in F., but possibly of a slightly later Flemish reprint. They are pleasing and full of life.

1. This belongs to lines 51 sqq. It is not reproduced in R.V. and not mentioned in Prien's edition on pp. 58–59.

2. This illustrates lines 91 sqq. and corresponds to a wood-cut in R.V. given at the beginning of Prien's edition and described by him on p. 65. This same wood-cut, but much mutilated (fol. 6a), occurs again in F., corresponding to the cut down text (ll. 162–87, on fol. 6b).

3. This illustrates lines 111 sqq. and has its counterpart in R.V. (as given in Wolff's edition on p. 137; see Prien's description on p. 68).

Original position and sequence of the leaves of F. This important question has been most carefully investigated and practically settled by Prien (in P.B.B. VIII, 16 sqq.). In re-constructing the lost portions with much ingenuity he rightly observed that in F. the usual arrangement is to give first the heading of a chapter (about four or five lines) followed by a wood-cut (filling a whole page), then a comparatively short gloss in prose, and finally the poetic text itself. See especially Chapter XXIII after line 161. The headings of new chapters are usually printed near the bottom of a page, thus rendering the whole of the next full page available for a wood-cut, while on the following page are placed the gloss and the beginning of the poetic text. For this reason after the heading of Chapter XXIV had been given half of a page remained empty, there not being enough room left for a full-page wood-cut.

It is not quite clear if there ever existed a slightly later reprint of the version represented by F., perhaps containing some small alterations of the text on which the Low German translation of 'Reinke de Vos' was based. This is not impossible, but seems unlikely; at any rate it would be unwise to make conjectures on the strength of the very scanty material at our disposal. Nor is it certain that the text of the Fragments is absolutely identical with that first published by Hinrek van Alckmer, as we are unable to prove definitely from the few leaves preserved, which belong exclusively to the earlier portion of the poem, that the text of this particular version was actually divided into four books as we know it was divided by Hinrek. It is, however, most probable that the Cambridge Reinaert Fragments actually represent the version made by Hinrek of 'Reinaerts Historie.' The chapters are neither quite the same as those met with in the Flemish chap-book (Antwerp, 1564) nor as those occurring in 'Reinke de Vos.' Some texts begin new chapters where others show no break. That R.V. is a translation from F. is proved, apart from other reasons, by the occurrence of a common mistake[1]. The text of F. corresponds to Chapters XVII to XX of the *First* book of R.V. It is much to be regretted that some leaves from the later parts of the Flemish book (as represented by F.) have not been preserved, as we should then know for certain if it was actually the one composed by Hinrek van Alckmer. It is expressly stated in the first Preface to R.V. (Lübeck, 1498), which is a translation from the Netherlandish, that Hinrek van Alckmer had divided his work into four books.

Importance of the Culemann Fragments. The F. are of the greatest importance in the literary tradition of the Beast Epic for two reasons :

(*a*) They are the immediate source of the Middle Low German 'Reinke de Vos' (Lübeck, 1498) which is the most important German version of the Reinaert story before Goethe; and

(*b*) They are one of the sources of the oldest Netherlandish chap-book (printed at Antwerp, 1564)[2].

REPRINTS OF THE CULEMANN FRAGMENTS UP TO 1926

1854(?) 1. *F. G. H. Culemann* printed them privately (no date; in 1854?) under the title 'Brokken eens ouden druks van den Reinaert in verzen,' 21 pages, size similar to that of the original ; only two illustrations (the best unmutilated ones) reproduced. On the left-hand pages are printed in large Gothic type Culemann's newly discovered fragments; on the right-hand pages, in parallel columns and in smaller Roman type, are printed: (on the left) the text of 'Reineke Vos' (after the original Lübeck edition as printed by Hoffmann von Fallersleben, Breslau, 1834, and (on the right) the text of 'Reinaert,' as given by Jacob Grimm, pp. 165 sqq.

---

[1] This has been shown by Prien in P.B.B. VIII, 51 sqq.; Reinke, l. 1458, repeating the obvious mistake made by F., l. 34; see pp. 32 and 33.   [2] See the diagram on p. xxii.

in his 'Reinhart Fuchs' edition. This Netherlandish text is, however, the older 'Reinaert' (I), and not the more important 'Reinaerts Historie.' Culemann misses out the two mutilated illustrations. His text contains a few misprints as well as the inconsistent spelling of F. Lines 91–110 are left out altogether without any mention of the omission (between pages 4 and 5). Only a single copy of this reprint is known. It is the one now preserved at Cambridge together with the original leaves of F. It is very probably only an incomplete and uncorrected set of proof-sheets. It is possible that another set of proofs was sent by Culemann to Hoffmann von Fallersleben, the first editor of F. who says in his Preface (p. 6): 'Einen getreuen Abdruck hat Herr Senator Culemann veranstaltet und ein Facsimile des Drucks und der Holzschnitte hinzugefügt und mir freundlichst die Benutzung gestattet, wofür ich ihm hiemit öffentlich Dank sage.' From this it is not clear if Hoffmann used merely a copy of the 'Brokken' or the original leaves as well, but it is very likely that in any case he did compare the two as Culemann's omission of ll. 91–110 does not occur in Hoffmann's edition.

2. *Hoffmann von Fallersleben.* 'Bruchstücke mittelniederländischer Gedichte, 1862 nebst Loverkens' (in 'Horae Belgicae,' xii, 1–15), Hannover, 1862. Not an absolutely accurate reproduction: slight omissions, alterations and normalising of spelling, punctuation. Only one of the three wood-cuts reproduced (No. 1 of the present edition).

3. *Friedrich Prien*, in his article published in Paul and Braune's 'Beiträge 1882 zur Geschichte der deutschen Sprache und Literatur,' viii (1882), 10–16. Very accurate (from a copy supplied by Mr G. A. S. Schneider. Prien had not himself seen F.).

4. *Friedrich Prien* in his very valuable edition of 'Reinke de vos,' revised 1887 with the utmost care, pp. 267–73. Only a few slight corrections were required and were published by me in the following year: Karl Breul, 'Zu den Cambridger Reinaertfragmenten' (in P.B.B. xiv (1888), 377–8). These corrections were completely ignored in the re-issue of the (unchanged) pages from Prien's edition which were simply tacked on to the new (1925) edition of 'Reinke de Vos' by

5. *Albert Leitzmann.* This edition is practically the same as No. 4, so far as 1925 the text is concerned, but Karl Voretzsch's Introduction on the later Beast Epic contributed to this edition is very welcome. In other respects, however, Prien's edition of 1887 is by no means superseded and still has an independent value by the side of the later (1925) edition. This is mainly due to his valuable Introduction.

Old French poem of the Court of the Lion
(branch 1—in older books xx—of the 'Roman de Renart')
after | 1160

Reinaert I
Old Flemish poem (not before 1235)
by two poets: Aernout and Willem

Reinardus Vulpes
Latin version by the monk Balduinus
(between 1267 and 1273 ?)

Reinaert II (Reinaerts Historie)
(about 1375)

Historie van Reinaert die Vos
Dutch prose, rimes of the original Reinaert II
still often noticeable
(Gouda 1479)
(reprinted Zwolle 1892)

(Delft 1485)
(reprinted Lübeck 1783)

Enlarged Verse reproduction
author: Hinrek van Alckmer
(printed: Antwerp, Leeu, 1487 (?))
four books, chapters, moralisations, illustrations,
only seven leaves (223 lines) preserved in
the (Cambridge) Culemann Fragments
(about 1480)

English translation
printed by Caxton
(London 1481)

Reynaert de Vos
Oldest prose Dutch chap-book
(Antwerp 1564)
(reprinted Paderborn
1876)

Reinke de Vos
Low German translation in four books
(Lübeck 1498)

Later Dutch
chap-books

High German translation
(Anonym. 1544)

Latin version
(by Hartmann
Schopper 1567)

Gottsched's High German prose
(1752)

Goethe's 'Reinecke Fuchs'
(1793)

BIBLIOGRAPHICAL NOTES

(Only the most important books and articles are mentioned in the following list)

1. ERNST VOIGT. *Ecbasis Captivi.* Das älteste Thierepos des Mittelalters. Straßburg, 1875. ('Quellen und Forschungen,' VIII.)
2. ERNST VOIGT. *Kleinere lateinische Denkmäler der Thiersage aus dem XII bis XIV Jahrhundert.* Straßburg, 1878. ('Q. u. F.,' XXV.)
3. ERNST VOIGT. *Ysengrimus.* Halle, 1884.
4. ERNST MARTIN. *Le Roman de Renart.* Strasbourg, 1882–1887. 3 vols.
5. KARL REISSENBERGER. *Reinhart Fuchs.* Halle, 1886, ²1908. (In Paul's 'Altdeutsche Textbibliothek,' vol. VII.)
6. GEORG BAESECKE. *Heinrichs des Glichezares Reinhart Fuchs.* Mit einem Beitrage von Karl Voretzsch. Halle, 1925. (In 'Altdeutsche Textbibliothek,' begründet von H. Paul, herausgegeben von G. Baesecke, vol. VII.)
7. ERNST MARTIN. *Reinaert.* Willems Gedicht Van den vos Reinaerde und die Umarbeitung und Fortsetzung Reinaerts Historie herausgegeben und erläutert. Paderborn, 1874. (See also J. W. Muller, *De oude en de jongere Bewerking van den Reinaert.* Amsterdam, 1888.)
8. ERNST MARTIN. *Neue Fragmente des Gedichtes Van den vos Reinaerde.* Straßburg, 1889. ('Q. u. F.,' LXV.)
9. J. W. MULLER. *Van den vos Reynarde.* Critisch uitgegeven door J. W. Muller. Gent, 1914. (Reprint of the critical text only: Utrecht, 1922.)
10. HOFFMANN VON FALLERSLEBEN. *Bruchstücke mittelniederländischer Gedichte, nebst Loverkens. I: Reinaert.* (In 'Horae Belgicae,' XII, 5–15.) Hannover, 1862.
11. *Die Historie van Reynart de Vos.* Chap-book in prose. Gouda, 1479, and Delft, 1485 (the former reprinted by J. W. Muller and M. Logeman, Zwolle, 1892; the latter reprinted by Suhl, Lübeck, 1783).
12. *Reynart de Vos.* Chap-book in prose. Antwerp, 1564. (New edition by Ernst Martin. Paderborn, 1876.)
13. HOFFMANN VON FALLERSLEBEN. *Reineke Vos.* Nach der Lübecker Ausgabe vom Jahre 1498. Mit Einleitung, Anmerkungen und Wörterbuch. Breslau, ¹1834, ²1852.
14. AUGUST LÜBBEN. *Reinke de Vos.* Nach der ältesten Ausgabe (Lübeck, 1498). Mit Einleitung, Anmerkungen und einem Wörterbuche. Oldenburg, 1867.

15. KARL SCHRÖDER. *Reinke de Vos*. (In 'Deutsche Dichtungen des Mittel-alters. Mit Wort- und Sacherklärungen,' vol. II.) Leipzig, 1872.

16. EUGEN WOLFF. *Reinke de Vos und satirisch-didaktische Dichtung*. (In Kürschner's 'Deutsche National-Litteratur,' vol. XIX.) Stuttgart, n.d.

17. FRIEDRICH PRIEN. *Reinke de vos*. (In Paul's 'Altdeutsche Textbiblio-thek,' vol. VIII.) Halle, 1887.

18. ALBERT LEITZMANN. *Reinke de vos*. Nach der Ausgabe von Friedrich Prien neu herausgegeben. Mit einer Einleitung von Karl Voretzsch. (In Paul-Baesecke's 'Altdeutsche Textbibliothek,' vol. VIII.) Halle, 1925.

19. FRIEDRICH PRIEN. *Zur Vorgeschichte des Reinke Vos*. (In Paul and Braune's 'Beiträge zur Geschichte der deutschen Sprache und Literatur,' vol. VIII, 1–53.) Halle, 1881.

20. KARL BREUL. *Zu den Cambridger Reinaertfragmenten*. (In Paul and Braune's 'Beiträge,' vol. XIV, 377–8.) Halle, 1888.

21. J. W. MULLER. *Mr Henric van Alcmaer*. (In the 'Tijdschrift voor Nederlandsche Taal- en Letterkunde,' VII (1887), 251–60.)

22. J. W. MULLER. *De twee dichters van Reinaert I*. (In the 'Tijdschrift voor N. T. en L.,' XXXI (1912), 177–275. Other literature is quoted by Karl Voretzsch in Leitzmann's ed. of *Reinke de vos*, Introd. XX, note.)

23. WILHELM SCHERER. *Jacob Grimm*. Berlin, ²1885, pp. 289 sqq.

24. WILHELM WACKERNAGEL. *Kleinere Schriften*. Leipzig, 1873. (Vol. II: 'Abhandlungen zur deutschen Litteratur-Geschichte,' pp. 234–326.)

25. JAN TEN BRINK. *De Litteratuur der Reinaert-Sagen*. (In 'Litterarische Schetsen en Kritieken,' III, 1–28.) Leyden, 1883.

26. KAARLE KROHN. *Bär (Wolf) und Fuchs*. (German translation by O. Hackmann.) Helsingfors, 1888.

27. LÉOPOLD SUDRE. *Les sources du Roman de Renard*. Paris, 1893. (Also in Petit de Julleville, *Histoire de la langue et de la littérature française des origines à 1900*, II, 14–56. Paris, 1896.)

28. LUCIEN FOULET. *Le Roman de Renard*. Paris, 1914. (In 'Bibliothèque des Hautes-Études, Sciences hist. et phil.,' no. 211. See Voretzsch.)

29. KARL VORETZSCH. *Einführung in das Studium der altfranzösischen Literatur*. Halle (Saale), ³1925, pp. 374 sqq.

30. KARL VORETZSCH. *Studien zu Tiersage und Tierepos*. (In 'Romanistische Arbeiten,' Heft 12, to be published some time next year. The treatise will contain a comparative study of *Ysengrimus, Roman de Renart* and *Reinhart Fuchs*.)

PART I

weet alhier den ghierighen gokeninck gheleert dat
hſ ſoe vᵹle niet rapen en ſal/dat hſ mids dien niet
en come in ſoedanighen gate daer hſ niet weder
wt comen en kan/twelck alhier oꝫ ꝫ bſden wolf
beteſkert weet want hſ ſinen buſck ſoe vol ghe⸗
gheten hadde dat hſ niet weder wt den gate ghe⸗
comen en konde aldaer hſ in ghecropē was Hier
weet oeck ghethoent dat die ſchalcken bedrieghen
heeren ende vrouwen.

ᵒ   ie coninck en is mſ niet ontgaen
         Jc hebbe hem dicke ſcande ghedaen
Ende ſine wiue der coninghinnen
Dat ſi ſpade ſal verwinnen
Sſ ſſn gheſcandalizeert bſ mſ
Noch hebbe ic daer ſegghic di
Pſengrine meer bedroghen
Dan ic ſoude ſegghen moghen
Dat icken oom hiet was beraet
Pſengcine die mi niet beſtaet
Jc maecten monick ter elmaren
Daer wſ beſde begheuen waren
Dat hem zeere woꝛt te pinen
Jc deden in die clockinghen
Binden beſde ſine voete
Dat luden dochte hem ſſn ſoe ſoete

2

. . . .
. . . .
. . . .
. . . .

wert alhier den ghierighen houelinck gheleert dat
hij soe vele niet rapen en sal/dat hi mids dien niet
en come in soedanighen gate daer hij niet weder
wt comen en kan/twelck alhier oe t byden wolf
beteykent wert want hij sinen buhck soe vol ghe=
gheten habbe dat hij niet weder wt den gate ghe=
comen en konde albaer hij in ghecropē was Hier
wert oeck ghethoent dat die schalcken bedrieghen
heeren ende vrouwen.

b   ie coninck en is mij niet ontgaen
     Ic hebbe hem dicke scande ghebaen
Ende sine wiue der coninghinnen
Dat si spade sal verwinnen
Sij sijn ghescandalizeert bĩ mij   5
Noch hebbe ic baer segghic bi
Ysengrine meer bedroghen
Dan ic soude segghen moghen
Dat icken oom hiet was beraet
Ysengrine die mi niet bestaet   10
Ic maecten monick ter elmaren
Daer wij beyde begheuen waren
Dat hem zeere wort te pinen
Ic beden in die clockinghen
Binden beyde sine voete   15
Dat luden dochte hem sijn soe soete

Oie gouoben woeⁱkvaer op in vaer
Ende waenden dattet die duuel ware
Sij liepen daer sij tluden hoorden
Ende eer hi cᴕnste in corten woerden
Gheseggben ic wil mij begheuen
Was hem wel na ghenomen tleuen
Ic dede hem of barnen thaer
Soe na den vel dat wel naer
Die zwaerde hem inden liue cramp
Sint leerde icken dat was sijn ramp
Visschen vanghen op eenen dach
Daer hi ontfinck menighen slach
Oec leyde icken tot spapen van bloys
In al dat lant van vermendoys
En woende gheen pape rijker
Dese pape had een spijker
Daer menich goet vet baeck in lach
Daer hi ontfinck menighen slach
Anden spijker had hi een gat
Ghemaect ende in dat
Dede ic pelegrine crupen
Daer hi cuntvleysch vant in cupen
Ende vetter baken alsoe vele
Dies liet hi gaen doer sijn kele
Soe groten hoop bouen maten
Dat hi wten seluen gaten

4

. . . .
. . . .
. . . .
. . . .

Diet hoorden worden daer bŷ in vare
Ende waenden dattet die duuel ware
Sij liepen daer ſij tluden hoorden
Ende eer hi conſte in corten woerden   20
Gheſegghen ic wil mij begheuen
Was hem wel na ghenomen tleuen
Ic dede hem of barnen thaer
Soe na den vel dat wel naer
Die zwaerde hem inden liue cramp   25
Sint leerde icken dat was ſijn ramp
Viſſchen vanghen op eenen dach
Daer hi ontfinck menighen ſlach
Oec leŷde icken tot ſpapen van bloŷs
In al dat lant van vermendoŷs   30
En woende gheen pape rijker
Deſe pape had een ſpijker
Daer menich goet vet baeck in lach
Daer hi ontfinck menighen ſlach
Anden ſpijker had hi een gat   35
Ghemaect ende in dat
Dede ic Iſegrine crupen
Daer hi runtvleŷſch vant in cupen
Ende vetter baken alſoe vele
Dies liet hi gaen doer ſijnkele   40
Soe groten hoop bouen maten
Dat hi wten ſeluen gaten

5

Dat hem sinen grooten buÿck benam
Doe moeste hi claghen sulck ghewin
Want daer hi hongherich quam in
En mocht hi sat niet comen wt
Jc ghinck ende maecte groot gheluut
Jn dat dorp ende groot gherochte
Nu hoert hoe ict daer toe brochte
Jc liep daer die pape sat
Ouer tafel ende at
Ende voer hem stont een capoen
Dat was een dat beste hoen
Datmen wiste in eenich lant
Dat hoen ic nmitter vaert pranc
Ende liep hene daer ic mochte
Doe maecte die pape groot gherochte
Ende riep lude vanc ende slach
Jc waen nÿe man dat wonder en sach
Dat mÿ een vos rooft mÿn hoenre
Jn mÿn buÿs wie sach ÿe coenre
Dief/ende daer ic sie toe
Sÿn tafelmes greep hi doe
Ende warp na mÿ mer ic ontvoer
Dat mes bleef steken inden vloer
Hÿ stack die tafel datse vloech
Ende volchde mÿ mit stemmen hoech
Roepende slach ende va
Jc vaste voren ende hi na
En mit hemluÿden een groot ghetal
Die mÿn quaetste meenden al   h iÿ

6

Niet wt en mochte
Dat hem finen grooten buhck benam
Doe moeste hi claghen fulck ghewin   45
Want daer hi hongherich quam in
En mocht hi fat niet comen wt
Jc ghinck ende maecte groot gheluut
In dat dorp ende groot gherochte
Nu hoert hoe ict daer toe brochte   50
Jc liep daer die pape fat
Ouer tafel ende at
Ende voer hem ftont een capoen
Dat was een dat befte hoen
Datmen wifte in eenich lant   55
Dat hoen ic mitter vaert pranc
Ende liep hene daer ic mochte
Doe maecte die pape gtoot gherochte
Ende riep lude vanc ende flach
Jc waen nhe man dat wonder en fach   60
Dat mij een vos rooft mijn hoenre
In mijn huhs wie fach he coenre
Dief/ende daer ic fie toe
Sijn tafelmes greep hi doe
Ende warp na mij mer ic ontvoer   65
Dat mes bleef fteken inden vloer
Hij ftack die tafel datfe vloech
Ende volchde mij mit ftemmen hoech
Roepende flach ende va
Jc vafte voren ende hi na   70
En mit hemluhden een groot ghetal
Die mijn quaetfte meenden al   h iij

7

ꝺoen iꝑ:aꝛ꜇ꝉ ꝑꞁa꜇꜇꜇ꞷꞩ ꞵꞵꞁ ꝺꞝꞇꞟ
Of this boerte dat ghi mÿ vertelt
Want wat ic soecke ic en vinde niet
Jc ſpꝛack oom wats v gheſchiet
Cruÿpt een luttel noch bat in
Men moet wel pinen om ghewin
Jc hebſe wech diere voꝛen ſaten
Dus croop hi in bouen maten
Dat hi die hoenren te verre ſochte
Jc ſach dat icken honen mochte
Ende ſtacken dat hi ouer voer
Ende quam gheuallen opten vlóe
Want die haenbalcke was ſmal
Ende gaf eenen groten val
Dat ſi ontſpꝛonghen alle dÿer ſlie꜇
Die daer bÿden viere laghen ſi rie꜇
Datter doer dat valdoꝛe gat
Gheuallen ware ſi en wiſten wat

℘ Hoe dat reÿnaert ſÿn biecht ſo
gende eñ ſlutēde:eñ hoe hÿ baer ͬ
baert te houe weert ghinck/eñ
inden weghe ghebuerde Dͬ

. . . .
. . . .
. . . .
. . . .

Doen sprack reynaert wij sijn vern
Of this boerte dat ghi mij vertelt
Want wat ic soecke ic en vinde niet   75
Ic sprack oom wats v gheschiet
Cruhpt een luttel noch dat in
Men moet wel pinen om ghewin
Ic hebse wech diere voren saten
Dus croop hi in bouen maten   80
Dat hi die hoenren te verre sochte
Ic sach dat icken honen mochte
Ende stacken dat hi ouer voer
Ende quam gheuallen opten vloe
Want die haenbalcke was smal   85
Ende gaf eenen groten val
Dat si ontspronghen alle bh̄er slie
Die daer bh̄den viere laghen si rie
Datter doer dat valdore gat
Gheuallen ware si en wisten wat   90

❡ Hoe dat reh̄naert sijn biecht is
gende eñ slutẽde: eñ hoe hij daer
baert te houe weert ghinck/eñ
inden weghe ghebuerde Da

ᵍ rimbert fach wel dit ghelaet
Ende feyde onfle onreyne vraet
Hoe laetty uwe ooghen omme gaen
Reynaert fprack neue dats mifdaen
Dat ghi mit uwe verlopende woort
Mÿ wt mÿn ghebede dus ftoort
Laet mÿ doch lefen een Pater nofter
Der hoenre zielen vanden cloofter
Ende den ganfen te ghenaden
Die ic dicke hebbe verraden
Doe icfe defe heylighe nonnen
Mit mÿnre lift heb of ghewonnen
Grimbaert balch hem mer reynaert
Had ymmer thooft ten hoenre waert
Tot fi quamen ter rechter ftraten
Die fi te voren hadden ghelaten
Daer keerden fi te houe waert
Och hoe feere beuede reynaert
Doe hÿ den houe began te naken
Daer hi feer in meende mifraken

¶ Hoe reynaert coemt in prefencie vandē coninc
die welke hi obedientelick toeniget eñ vindet daer
elkerlÿck ouer hem claghende Dat.xxÿ.capittel

14

. . . .
. . . .
. . . .
. . . .

g   rimbert ſach wel dit ghelaet
    Ende ſeyde vuʒle onreʒne vraet
Hoe laettʒ uwe ooghen omme gaen
Reʒnaert ſpracf neue dats miſdaen
Dat ghi mit uwe verlopende woort   95
Mij wt mijn ghebede bus ſtoort
Laet mij doch leſen een Pater noſter
Der hoenre zielen vanden clooſter
Ende den ganſen te ghenaden
Die ic dicfe hebbe verraden   100
Doe icſe deſe heʒlighe nonnen
Mit mijnre liſt heb of ghewonnen
Grimbaert balch hem mer reʒnaert
Hab ʒmmer thooft ten hoenre waert
Tot ſi quamen ter rechter ſtraten   105
Die ſi te voren habden ghelaten
Daer feerden ſi te houe waert
Och hoe ſeere beuede reʒnaert
Doe hij den houe began te nafen
Daer hi ſeer in meende miſrafen   110

℃ Hoe reʒnaert coemt in preſencie vanbẽ coninc
die welfe hi obedientelicf toeniget eñ vindet baer
elferlijcf ouer hem claghende Dat .xxij. capittel

15

Nochtans dede hi als die onueruaerde
Ende liet hem bat dan hem was
Hi ghinck mit sinen neue den das
Cierliken doer die hoochste strate
Alsoe moedich van ghelate.
Als of hi sconincs sone waer
Ende hi oec van enen haer
Jeghen nyemant en hadde misdaen
Voer nobel den coninck ghinck hi staen
Midden inden heeren rinck
Ende seyde god die alle dinck
Gheboot die gheue o coninck heer
Langhe blyscap ende groot eer
Ic gruet o heer ic hebbe recht
Ten hadde nye coninck enen knecht
Soe ghetrouwe ieghen hem
Als ic o ye was ende noch ben
Dat ic oeck dicke bin werden anschyn
Nochtan sulcke die hier syn
Souden my gheerne o hulde rouen
Mit loghen woudys hem ghelouen
Mer neen ghi niet god moets o lonen
Het en betaemt niet der cronen
Dat ghi den schalcken ende den fellen
Te licht ghelouet van dat si tellen
Nochtan wil icx gode claghen
Daer isser te vele in onsen daghen
Die mitter looshept die sy konnen
Die voerderhant nv hebben ghewonnen

16

Nochtans bebe hi als die onuervaerde
Ende liet hem bat dan hem was
Hi ghinck mit sinen neue den bas
Cierliken doer die hoochste strate
Alsoe moedich van ghelate   115
Als of hi sconincs sone waer
Ende hi oec van enen haer
Jeghen nyemant en habbe misdaen
Voer nobel den coninck ghinck hi staen
Midden inden heeren rinck   120
Ende seyde god die alle dinck
Gheboot die gheue v coninck heer
Langhe blijscap ende groot eer
Ic gruet v heer ic hebbe recht
Ten habbe nye coninck enen knecht   125
Soe ghetrouwe ieghen hem
Als ic v ye was ende noch ben
Dat ic oeck dicke bin werden anschijn
Nochtan sulcke die hier sijn
Souden mij gheerne v hulde rouen   130
Mit loghen woudijs hem ghelouen
Mer neen ghi niet god moets v lonen
Het en betaemt niet der cronen
Dat ghi den schalcken ende den fellen
Te licht ghelouet van dat si tellen   135
Nochtan wil icz gode claghen
Daer isser te vele in onsen daghen
Die mitter loosheyt die sij konnen
Die vorderhant nv hebben ghewonnen

Ouer al in heren houen
Dat sy soe verre conten bouen
Die schalcke syn in dien gheboren
Dat sy den goeden beraden toren
Dat wreke god an haer leuen
Ende moet hem sulck loon gheuen
Als sy van rechte wel syn waert
Die coninck sprack an reynaert
Onreyne onsle lose druut
Hoe wel coendy uwen saluut
Maer ten baet v niet een kaf
Coemt uwes smeekens af
Ic en worde by smeeken niet v vrient
Dat ghi my dicke wel hebt ghedient
Dat wort v no te rechte ghegouden
Ghi hebt oec wel den vrede ghehouden
Dien ic gheboot ende hebbe ghesworen
Owy wat heb ic al verloren
Sprack cantecleer aldaer hy stont
Die coninck sprack hout uwen mont
Her cantecleer ende laet my spreken
Ic moet antwoerden sine treken

℩ Hoe dat die coninck reynaert zeere confu
selyck en wredelyck toe spreect om der groo
ter quade felle daden daer hy of beclaecht is/
en hoe dat hem reynaert weder verantwoert
soe hi best kan Dat.xxiij.capittel

18

Ouer al in heren houen   140

Dat sij soe verre comen bouen

Die schalcke sijn in dien gheboren

Dat sij den goeden beraden toren

Dat wreke god an haer leuen

Ende moet hem sulck loon gheuen   145

Als sij van rechte wel sijn waert

Die coninck sprack an reynaert

Onreyne vuyle lose druut

Hoe wel coendy uwen saluut

Maer ten baet v niet een kaf   150

Coemt uwes smeekens af

Ic en worde by smeeken niet v vrient

Dat ghi mij dicke wel hebt ghedient

Dat wort v nv te rechte ghegouden

Ghi hebt oec wel den vrede ghehouden   155

Dien ic gheboot ende hebbe ghesworen

O wij wat heb ic al verloren

Sprack cantecleer aldaer hij stont

Die coninck sprack hout uwen mont

Her cantecleer ende laet mij spreken   160

Ic moet antwoerden sine treken

℘ Hoe dat die coninck reynaert zeere confu
selijck eñ wredelijk toe spreect om der groo
ter quade felle daden daer hij of beclaecht is/
eñ hoe dat hem reynaert weder verantwoert
soe hi best kan Dat .xxiij. capittel

20

enichte vanden claghers voerder be
ɔɟl gheuanghen.
ef ſprack hɟ fel reɟnaert
ɲ mɟ lief hebt ende waert
ɩden lachter mɟn
n ghedaen aenſchɟn
ɩbert ende bꝛune
loedich is ſɟn crune
ɩt vele ſchelden
ɩe ʋ kele ſalt ontghelden
ɑl op eene wɟle
er xpꝛiſte kɟle
naert heete ende of bꝛune
edich heeft die cruɲe
ɩ wat beſcaet mɟ dat
ɟts honich at
ɟie doꝛper tachter dede
bꝛune ſoe ſtarcke lɩde
ɩghen of verſpꝛoken
ɩt hɩ hadt ghewꝛoken
ɩ in dat water
e tɟbaert die kater
chde ende wel ontfinck
n ſtelen ghinck
ɩ huɟs ſonder minen raet
ɟie pape dede quaet

enichte vanden claghers voerber be
vijl gheuanghen.
ef fprack hij fel reħnaert
gi mij lief hebt enbe waert
ben lachter mijn
n ghebaen aenfchijn   165
bert enbe brune
loebich is fijn crune
et vele fchelben
ke v kele falt ontghelben
al op eene wijle   170
er xprifte fijle
naert heere enbe of brune
ebich heeft bie crune
wat befcaet mij bat
ħts honich at   175
bie borper tachter bebe
brune foe ftarcke lebe
ghen of verfproken
et hi habt ghewroken
in bat water   180
e tħbaert bie kater
chbe enbe wel ontfinck
n ftelen ghinck
huħs fonber minen raet
bie pape bebe quaet   185

Bylode soude ic des ontghelden
Hoe mostick myn gheluc wel schelden
Niet daer by her coninck lyon
Wat ghi wilt dat moechdy doen
Ende ghebieden ouer my
Hoe goet hoe claer myn saxe sy
Ghi moecht my vromen ende scaden
Wildy my sieden ofte braden
Ofte hanghen ofte blenden
Ic en mach v niet ontwenden
Wy syn alle in uwen bedwanck
Ghi syt starck ende ic bin cranck
Myn hulp is cleyn die uwe is groot
Voerwaer al sloechdi my doot
Dat waer v eene crancke wrake
Recht in deser seluer sprake
Spranck op bellyn den ram
Ende syn moeye die mit hemquam
Dat was dame olewy
Bellyn sprack nv toe gaen wy
Alle voert mit onser claghen
Brune spranck op mit sinen maghen
Ende tybert syn ghesselle
Ende pelegrim die snelle
Die haze ende dat euerzwyn
Elck wilde in die claghe syn
Panthel die kemel ende bruneel
Die gans dat wezel ende tlampreel
Boudwin den ezel borreel den stier

24

Bßlode foude ic des ontghelden
Soe moſtick mijn gheluc wel ſchelden
Niet daer bß her coninck lßon
Wat ghi wilt dat moechbß doen
Ende ghebieden ouer mij   190
Hoe goet hoe claer mijn ſafe ſij
Ghi moecßt mij vromen ende ſcaden
Wildß mij ſieden ofte braden
Ofte hanghen ofte blenden
Ic en mach v niet ontwenden   195
Wij ſijn alle in uwen bedwanck
Ghi ſijt ſtarck ende ic bin cranck
Mijn hulp is cleßn die uwe is groot
Voerwaer al ſloecßbi mij doot
Dat waer v eene crancke wrake   200
Recht in deſer ſeluer ſprake
Spranck op bellijn den ram
Ende ſijn moeße die mit ßem quam
Dat was dame olewij
Bellijn ſprack nv toe gaen wij   205
Alle voert mit onſer claghen
Brune ſpranck op mit ſinen maghen
Ende tßbert ſijn gheſelle
Ende ßſegrim die ſnelle
Die ßaze ende dat euerzwijn   210
Elck wilde in die claghe ſijn
Panthel die femel ende bruneel
Die gans dat wezel ende tlampreel
Boudwin den ezel borreel den ſtier

Dat herntel die wesel waren oeck hier
Cantecler ende sijn kinder
Claechden seer haren hinder
Ende maecten groot wederslach
Dat troeseel een cleen besach
Liep oeck mede in deser scare
Alle dese ghinghen openbare
Voer haren heere den conick staen
Ende deden den vos reynaert vaen

¶ Hoe die coninck te recht sittet ende gheeft
die sentencie datmen reynaert vanghen sou
de ende byder kelen hanghen Dat.xxiiij.capittel.

Dat hermel die wesel waren oeck hier   215
Cantecler ende sijn kinder
Claechden seer haren hinder
Ende maecten groot wederslach
Dat troeseel een cleen beiach
Liep oeck mede in deser scare   220
Alle dese ghinghen openbare
Voer haren heere den conick staen
Ende deden den vos reynaert vaen

℄ Hoe die coninck te recht sittet ende gheeft
die sentencie datmen reynaert vanghen sou
de en̄ byder kelen hanghē Dat .xxiiij. capittel.

PART II

wert alhier den ghierighen houelincl
gheleert, dat hij soe vele niet rapen en sal
dat hi mids dien niet en come in soedanighe¤
gate daer hij niet weder wt comen en kan
twelck alhier oeck byden wolf beteyken¤
wert want hij sinen buyck soe vol gheghete¤
hadde dat hij niet weder wt den gate ghe
comen en konde aldaer hij in ghecropen was
Hier wert oeck ghethoent dat die schalcke¤
bedrieghen heeren ende vrouwen.

Die coninc enis mi niet ontgaen.
ic heb hem dicke schande ghedaen
1515 ende sinen wive der coninghinne,
dat si spade sel verwinnen.
si sijn ghescandaliseert bi mi.
noch heb ic, dat segghic di,
Isengrine meer bedroghen
1520 dan ic soude segghen moghen.
dat icken oom hiet, dat was verraet,
Isengrine die mi niet enbestaet.
ic maecten monic ter Elmaren,
daer wi beide begheven waren:
1525 dat hem sere wart te pinen.
ic dede hem an die cloclinen
binden beide sine voete.
dat luden docht hem wesen so soete,

'Die coninck en is mij niet ontgaen :
ic hebbe hem dicke scande ghedaen
ende sinen wive der coninghinnen,
dat si spade sal verwinnen;
5 sij sijn ghescandalizeert by mij.
Noch hebbe ic, dat segghic di,
Ysengrine meer bedroghen
dan ic soude segghen moghen.
Dat icken oom hiet, was beraet :
10 Ysengrine die mi niet bestaet.
Ic maecten monick ter Elmaren,
dar wi beide begheven waren,
dat hem zeere wort te pinen.
Ic deden an die cloclinen
15 binden beyde sine voete.
Dat luden dochte hem sijn soe soete

30

...Dat drydde, dat hyr de poete menet, dar he van deme wulue secht, dat he so vele ath, dat he vth deme ghathe nycht wedder konde komen sath, dar he hungerych in quam, darby syn to vorstande alle de, dede komen by eyn leen efte prouene, voghedye, efte wat yd sy, dar rente efte vordeel to boren is, edder ok eyn ander ghyryger, de wes to hope sleyt, vnnochsam edder ane nôghe, vnde alleyne syn ghewyn socht vnde syne bathe, vnde nycht der meenheyt......dyt menet he dar, dar Reynke secht, dat he heft ghedaen vntruwe vnde schande synem heren, deme konnynge, vnde der konnyngynnen.

(From the Gloss to I, 17, pages 62–63)

'De konnynck en is my nicht entghaen,
Ik hebbe em vaken schande ghedan,'
1415 Sprak Reynke, 'vnde ok der konnyginnen,
Dat se spade wyl vorwynnen;
Se synt beyde gheschendet by my.
Noch hebbe ik dar to, dat segge ik dy,
Isegrym den wulff gheschendet myt vlyt,
1420 Dat al to seggen neme vele tyd.
He is nicht myn om, wol heet ik en so,
He horet my altes nichtes to.
Id gheschach eyns, des is wol ses yar,
He quam to my to der Elemar
1425 In dat kloster, dar ik was
Begheuen vp dat sulue pas.
He bath, dat ik em helpen scholde,
Wente he dar ok monnyck werden wolde.
He meende, dat were van synen dyngen,
1430 Vnde beghunde myt der klocken to klyngen;
Dat lûdent duchte em wesen so soethe.

31

dat hijt immer woude leren.
1530 mer dat was luttel te sijnre ere:
want hi lude so utermaten
dat alle die lude bi der straten,
diet hoorden, worden daer of in vare
ende waenden dattet die duvel ware.
1535 si liepen daer sijt luden hoorden.
ende eer hi conste in corten woorden
ghesegghen 'ic wil mi begheven,'
was hem wel na ghenomen tleven.
ic dede hem of bernen thaer
1540 so na den vel dat wel naer
die swaerde hem aen den live cramp.
sint leerde ic hem (dat was sijn ramp)
vische vanghen op enen dach,
daer hi ontfinc menighen slach.
1545 ooc leidicken tes papen van Blois.
in al dat lant van Vermendois
enwoonde gheen pape riker.
dese pape had enen spiker,
daer menich goet vet bake in lach,
1550 daer ic mi dicke op te saden plach.
aen den spiker had ic een gat
selve ghemaect, ende in dat
dede ic Isengrine crupen,
daer hi rintvleisch vant in cupen
1555 ende vetter baken also veel.
dies liet he gaen door sijn keel
so groten hoop boven maten
dat hi uten selven gate

. . . .
. . . .
. . . .
. . . .
diet hoorden worden daer by in vare
ende waenden dattet die duvel ware.
Sie liepen daer sij tluden hoorden.
20 Ende eer hi conste in corten woorden
ghesegghen: 'Ic wil mi begheven,'
was hem wel na ghenomen tleven.
Ic dede hem of barnen thaer
soe na den vel, dat wel naer
25 die zwaerde hem in den live cramp.
Sint leerde icken—dat was sijn ramp—
visschen vanghen op eenen dach,
daer hi ontfinck menighen slach.
Oec leyde icken tot spapen van Bloys.
30 In al dat lant van Vermendoys
enwoonde gheen pape rijker.
Dese pape had een spijker
daer menich goet vet baeck in lach,
daer hi ontfinck menighen slach.
35 An den spijker had ic een gat
selve ghemaect, ende in dat
dede ic Ysegrine crupen,
daer hi rintvleysch vant in cupen
ende vetter baken alsoe vele.
40 Dies liet hi gaen doer sijn kele
so groten hoop boven maten,
dat hi wten selven gaten

Ik leet em bynden beyde vȯthe
An den klockreep na syneme wyllen,
Vp dat he synen lusten mochte styllen
1435 Vnde dat lůdent wol mochte leren.
Men dyt quam em to klenen eren;
Wente he ludde so sere vtermaten,
Dat alle dat volk by der straten
Weren alle in groter vare.
1440 Se meneden, de duuel were dare,
Vnde lepen, dar se dat lůdent horden;
Vnde eer he konde in korten worden
Seggen: 'ik wyl my hir begheuen,'
Hadden se em vyl na ghenomen syn leuen.
1445 He bath my, dat ik en scholde eren
Vnde dat ik em lethe eyne platten scheren;
Dar suluest to der Elemar
Leet ik em affbernen bouen dat haer
So seer, dat em de swarde kramp.
1450 Vaken krech he van my den ramp.
Ik lerde em vyssche vangen vp eynen dach,
Dar de ok enttenck mannygen slach.
Ik leydede en eyns in Gůleker lant
To eynes papen hus seer wol bekant;
1455 Dar suluest en was neen pape ryker.
Desse hadde eynen langen spyker,
Dar mannych specksyde ynne lach,
Dar he entfenck mannygen slach;
Dar to was in deme spyker noch
1460 Versch fles ghesolten in eynen troch.
Isegrym brack dorch de want eyn gath,
Vp dat he flesches mochte ethen sath.
Ik heth en vry krupen dar in,
Ik wolde en schenden, dat was myn syn.
1465 He ath so vele vthermathe,
Dat he vth deme suluen ghathe

niet uut enmocht, daer hi in quam,
1560 dat hem sijn grote buuc benam.
doe most hi claghen sulc ghewin:
want daer hi hongherich quam in,
enmocht hi sat niet comen uut.
ic ghinc ende maecte groot gheluut
1565 in dat dorp ende groot gherochte.
nu hoort, hoe ict daer toe brochte.
ic liep daer die pape sat
over tafel ende at
ende voor hem stont een capoen.
1570 dat was een dat beste hoen
dat men wist in enich lant.
dat hoen ic mitter vaert prant
ende liep heen al dat ic mochte.
doe maecte die pape groot gherochte
1575 ende riep lude 'vanc ende slach!
ic waen nie man dat wonder ensach
dat mi een vos rooft mine hoenre
in mijn huus (wie sach ie coenre
dief!) ende daer ic sie toe.'
1580 sijn tafelmes greep hi doe
ende warp na mi. mer ic ontvoer:
dat mes bleef steken in den vloer.
hi stiet die tafel dat si vlooch
ende volchde mi mit stemmen hooch
1585 roepende 'slach ende va!'
ic liep voor ende hi na,
ende mit hem luden een groot ghetal
die mijn quaetste meenden al.

niet wt enmochte daar he inquam
dat hem sinen grooten buyck benam.
45 Doe moeste hi claghen sulck ghewin:
want daer hi hongherich quam in,
enmocht hi sat niet comen wt.
Ic ghinck ende maecte groot gheluut
in dat dorp ende groot gherochte.
50 Nu hoert, hoe ict daer toe brochte!
Ic liep dar die pape sat
over tafel ende at,
ende voer hem stont een capoen;
dat was een dat beste hoen
55 dat men wiste in eenich lant.
Dat hoen ic mitter vaert prant
ende liep hene daer ic mochte.
Doe maecte die pape groot gherochte
ende riep lude: 'Vanc ende slach!
60 Ic waen nye man dat wonder ensach
dat mij een vos rooft mijn hoenre
in mijn huys—wie sach ie coenre
dief!—ende daer ic sie toe!'
Sijn tafelmes greep hi doe
65 ende warp na mij; mer ic ontvoer:
dat mes bleef stecken in den vloer.
Hij stack die tafel datse vloech
ende volchde mij mit stemmen hoech
roepende: 'Slach ende va!'
70 Ic vaste voren ende hi na,
ende mit hem luyden een groot ghetal
die mijn quaetste meenden al.

Nicht komen konde, dar he in quam,
Dat em syn grote buek benam.
Do moste he klagen solk ghewyn;
470 Wente dar he hungerich sus quam in,
En mochte he sath nicht komen vth.
Ik ghynck vnde makede groet gheluth
In dat dorp vnde groet gherochte,
Vp dat ik en to plasse brochte.
475 Ik leep, dar de pape sath
Ouer tafelen vnde ath,
Vnde vor em stunt eyn kappon
Ghebraden, eyn so vetten hon.
Ik spranck to myt der hast
480 Vnde nam dat hoen vnde leep do vast.
De pape makede groet gherochte,
He leep my na, al dat he mochte;
Vnvorwarynges he vmmetoch
De tafel, dat se henne vloch.
485 Dyt schach al an synen danck;
Dar lach spyse vnde dranck.
He reep: 'Sla, warp, vange vnde steck!'
Do vel de pape in den dreck.
Al de dar quemen, de repen: 'Sla!'
490 Ik leep vor vnde se my dat na.
Des volkes wart vele in deme tal,
De myn argeste meenden al.
De pape dat grotste rochte dreff,
He reep: 'We sach ye konre deeff?'

Doe sprac hi 'Reinaert, wi sijn vermelt,

of tis boerte dat ghi mi telt:
want wat ic soeke, ic envinde niet.'
1640 ic sprac 'oom, wats u ghesciet?
cruupt een luttel noch bet in:
men moet wel pinen om ghewin.
ic hebse wech, diere saten voren.'
dus liet hem Isegrijn verdoren
1645 dat hi die hoenre te verre sochte.
ich sach dat icken honen mochte
ende stieten dat hi over voer
ende quam ghevallen op die vloer,
(want die haenbalc was smal)
1650 ende gaf enen groten val,
dat si ontspronghen die daer sliepen.
die bi den viere laghen, si riepen
datter door dat valdoregat
ghevallen waer, si enwisten wat.

Doe sprack hi: 'Reynaert, wij sijn
   ver*melt*,
of tis boerte dat ghi mij vertelt:
75 want wat ic soecke, ic en vinde niet.'
Ic sprack: 'Oom, wats u gheschiet?
Cruypt een luttel noch bat in:
men moet wel pinen om ghewin.
Ic hebse wech diere voren saten.'
80 Dus croop hi in boven maten,
dat hi die hoenren te verre sochte.
Ic sach dat icken honen mochte
ende stacken dat hi over voer
ende quam ghevallen opten vlo*er*,
85 (want die haenbalcke was smal)
ende gaf eenen groten val,
dat si ontspronghen alle dyer slie*pen*.
Die daer byden viere laghen, si rie*pen*
datter doer dat valdoregat
90 ghevallen ware, si enwisten wat.

❧ Hoe dat Reynaert sijn biecht
*Grim*baert *seg*gende en*de* slute*nde*: end
hoc hij daer *mit Grim*baert te hov
weert ghinck en*de* in den wegh
ghebuerde. Da*t xxj. capittel.*

555 Do swor he dure by syner ere:
'Wy syn vormeldet, dat vruchte ik sere.
Hir vynde ik van honren nicht eynen bytten.'
Ik sprack: 'De hir vore plegen to sytten,
De hebbe ik vuste wech ghenomen.
560 Men wylle wy schaffen vnsen vromen,
Wy moghen nicht vordroten syn
Vnde mothen deper krepen in.'
De balke was smal bouen der dore,
Dar wy vp kropen; men he was vore.
565 De wyle he sus de honre sochte,
Sach ick, dat ik en hŏnen mochte:
Ick krop to rugge wedder vth,
Dat venster vel to ouerlud,
Do ick de stutteklyncken loßbrack.
570 Dar van Ysegrym so sere vorschrack,
Dat he vel eynen swaren val
Van deme balken, wente he was smal.
Se worden vorveret, de dar slepen;
De by deme vŭre legen, se repen,
575 Dat dorch des hogen vensters gath
Ghevallen were, se wusten nicht wat.

Grimoaert sach wel dat ghelaet
ende seide 'vule onreine vraet,
hoe laetti u oghen omme gaen!'
Reinaert sprac 'neve, tis misdaen
1755 dat ghi mit u overlopende woort
mi uut mijn ghebede dus stoort.
laet mi doch lesen een pater noster
der hoenre sielen van den clooster
ende den gansen te ghenaden
1760 die ic dicke heb verraden,
doe icse desen heilighen nonnen
mit mijnre list heb of ghewonnen.'
Grimbaert balch hem: mer Reinaert
had altijt thooft ten hoenre waert,
1765 tent si quamen ter rechter straten
die si te voren hadden ghelaten:
daer keerden si te hove waert.
och, hoe sere beefde Reinaert,
doe hi den hove began te naken,
1770 daer hi sere in waende misraken.

Grimbaert sach wel dit ghelaet
ende seyde: 'Vuyle onreyne vraet,
hoe laetty uwe ooghen omme gaen!'
Reynaert sprack: 'Neve, dats misdaen,
95 dat ghi mit uwe verlopende woort
mij wt mijn ghebede dus stoort.
Laet mij doch lesen een Pater noster
der hoenre zielen van den clooster
ende den gensen te ghenaden
100 die ic dicke hebbe verraden,
doe icse dese heylighe nonnen
mit mijnre list heb of ghewonnen.'
Grimbaert balch hem: mer Reynaert
had ymmer thooft ten hoenre waert,
105 tot si quamen ter rechter straten,
die si te voren hadden ghelaten:
daer keerden si te hove waert.
Och, hoe seere bevede Reynaert,
doe hij den hove began te naken,
110 daer hi seer in meende misraken.

❡ Hoc Reynaert coemt in presencie
van den coninc die welke hi obedientelick toeniget en*de* vindet daer elkerlijck
over hem claghende. Dat .xxjj. capittel

1665 Grymbart sach wol dyt ghelaet.
He sprack: 'O Reynke, vnreyne vraet,
Wo lathe gy yuwe oghen vmme ghaen!'
Reynke sprack: 'Om, dat is mysghedaen,
Dat gy myt yuwen vorlopenden worden
1670 My sus vth myneme bede vorstorden.
Latet my doch lesen eyn pater noster
Der honre selen van deme kloster
Vnde ock den gansen, en al tho gnaden,
Der ick gantz vele hebbe vorraden,
1675 De ick dessen hylgen nunnen
Myt myner lyst hebbe affghewunnen.'
Grymbart swech, men de vos Reynart
Hadde yummer dat hŏuet to den honren wert,
Wente dat se quemen tor rechten straten,
1680 De se to voren hadden ghelaten.
To hant wart Reynke seer bedrŏuet,
Meer wan yennich rechte lŏuet,
Do he sach den hoff, des konnynges pallas,
Dar he int hogeste vorklaget was.

℡ Wo Reynke kumpt in den hoft vor den konninck, deme he otmodichlyk tonyget, vnde vyndet
dar welke, de ouer en klaghen. Dat xix capittel.

39

Nochtan dede hi als die onvervaerde
ende gheliet hem bet dan hem was.
1780 hi ghinc mit sinen neve den das
herde fierlic door die hoochste strate
also moedich van ghelate
als of hi sconincs sone ware
ende hi ooc van enen hare
1785 jeghen niemen enhad misdaen.
voor Nobel den coninc ghinc hi staen
midden in der heren rinc
ende seide 'god die alle dinc
gheboot, die gheve u, coninc here,
1790 langhe bliscap ende groot ere.
ic groet u, here, ic hebbes recht.
tenhad nie coninc enen cnecht
so ghetrouwe teghen hem,
als ic u ie was ende noch bem.
1795 tis dicke worden aenschijn.
nochtan sulke die hier sijn
souden mi gherne u hulde roven
mit loghen, woudijs hem gheloven.
mer neen, ghi niet, god moets u lonen.
1800 het enbetaemt ooc niet der cronen
datsi den scalken ende den fellen
te licht ghelooft van dat si tellen.
nochtan wil ics gode claghen:
daer isser te veel in onsen daghen
1805 die mitter boosheit die si connen
die vorder hant nu hebben ghewonnen

Nochtan dede hi als die onvervaerde
ende liet hem bat dan hem was.
Hi ghinck mit sinen neve den das
Cierliken doer die hoochste strate
115 alsoe moedich van ghelate
als of hi sconincs sone waer
ende hi oec van enen haer
jeghen nyemant en hadde misdaen.
Vor Nobel den coninck ghinck hi staen
120 midden in den heeren rinck
ende seyde: 'God, die alle dinck
gheboot, die gheve u, coninck heer,
langhe blijscap ende groot eer.
Ic gruet u, heer, ic hebbe recht.
125 Ten hadde nye coninck enen knecht
so getrouwe ieghen hem
als ic u ye was ende noch ben.
Dat ic oeck dicke bin worden anschijn.
Nochtan sulcke die hier sijn
130 souden mij gheerne u hulde roven
mit loghen, woudijs hem gheloven,
mer neen, ghi niet, god moets u lonen
Het enbetaemt niet der cronen
dat ghi den schalcken ende den fellen
135 te licht ghelovet van dat si tellen.
Nochtan wil ics gode claghen:
Daer isser te vele in onsen daghen,
die mitter loosheyt, die sij konnen,
die vorderhant nu hebben ghewonnen

Des dede he alze de vnvorverde.
Myt syneme ome, deme greuynck,
Drystichlyken he so vor syck ghynck
1695 Tzyrlyken dorch de hogesten strate,
Alzo modich van ghelate,
Efte he were des konnynges sone
Vnde eft he nemande vp eyne bone
Edder sus nemande hadde myßghedaen.
1700 Vor Nobel den konninck ghynck he staen
Manckt de heren in den pallas
Vnde helt syck beth, wan eme was.
   He sprack: 'Eddele konnynck, gnedyge here,
Dorch yuwe eddelheyt vnde dorch yuwe ere
1705 Ik bydde, dat gy my horen to recht.
Id en hadde ny here so truwen knecht,
Alze ik yuwer vorstlyken gnaden byn,
Wo wol dat der vele hir syn,
De my yuwe fruntschop menen berouen
1710 Myt loggen, wan gy en des wolden louen.
Men yuwe rad is vroet, erst vnde lest;
Gy louen nicht draden, dat is dat best,
Wat yw desse valschen alle vore lesen
Myt leghen vnde dregen in mynem affwesen.
1715 Se hathen, dat ik yuwe beste mene
Vnde yw alle tyd truwychlyken dene.'

over al in heren hoven,
dat si so verre sijn comen boven.
die schalke sijn in dien gheboren
1810 dat si den goeden beraden torcn.
dat wreke god aen haer leven
ende moet hem sulken loon gheven
als si van rehte wel sijn waert.'
die coninc sprac 'ay Reinaert,
1815 onreine vule bose druut,
hoe wel condi uwen saluut!
mer tenbaet u niet een caf.
coomt uwes smekens af!
ic enworde bi smeken niet u vrient.
1820 dat ghi mi dicke hebt ghedient,
dat wort u nu te rechte ghegouden.
ghi hebt den vrede wel ghehouden
dien ic gheboot ende had ghesworen.'
'o wi, wat heb ic al verloren'
1825 sprac Cantecleer aldaer hi stont.
die coninc sprac 'hout uwen mont,
her Cantecleer, ende laet mi spreken.
ic moet antwoorden sinen treken.'

140 over al in heren hoven,
dat si so verre comen boven.
Die schalcke sijn in dien gheboren,
dat sij den goeden beraden toren.
Dat wreke god an haer leven
145 ende moet hem sulck loon gheven
als sij van rechte wel sijn waert.'
Die coninck sprack: 'Ay Reynaert,
onreyne vuyle lose druut!
Hoe wel coendy uwen saluut!
150 Maer tenbaet u niet een kaf.
Coemt uwes smeekens af!
Ic en worde by smeeken niet u vrien
Dat ghi mij dicke wel hebt ghedient,
dat wort u nu te rechte ghegouden.
155 Ghi hebt oec wel den vrede ghehoude
dien ic gheboot ende hebbe ghesworen
'O wij, wat heb ic al verloren!'
Sprack Cantecleer aldaer hij stont.
Die coninck sprack: 'Hout uwen mon
160 her Cantecleer, ende laet mij spreken
Ic moet antwoerden sine treken.'

❦ Hoe dat die coninck Reynaert zeer
confuselijk en*de* wredelijk toespreec
om der grooter quade felle daden dae
hij of beclaecht is, ende hoe dat hem
Reynaert weder verantwoert soe hi bes
can. Dat .xxiii. capittel.

1717 De konnynck sprack: 'Swyget, latet aff!
Juwe smekent helpet yw nicht eyn kaff.
Juwe vndaet wert yw nu vorgolden,
1720 Wo gy den vrede hebben gheholden,
Den ik gheboet vnde hebben ghesworen.
Hir steyt de hane, de heft vorloren
Syn slechte; o, valsche vntruwe deeff!'

'quaet dief,' sprac he, 'fel Reinaert!
1830 dat ghi mi lief hebt ende waert,
dat hebdi in den lachter mijn
minen boden ghedaen aenschijn.
aen aerm man Tibeert ende Brune,
dien noch al bloedich is die crune.
1835 ic enwil niet veel schelden:
mer ic denke u kele salt ontghelden
noch heden al op ene wile.'
'nomen pater christe file,'
sprac Reinaert 'here, ende of Brune
1840 noch al bloedich heeft die crune,
here coninc, wat bestaet mi dat,
of hi Lanfreits honich at
ende hem die dorper lachter dede?
noch heeft Brune so starke lede,
1845 was hi ghesleghen of versproken,
ware hi goet, hi hadt ghewroken,
eer hi quam in dat water,
efter van Tibaert die cater,
dien ic herberchde ende wel ontfinc,
1850 of hi uut om stelen ghinc
tot des papen huus, sonder minen raet,
ende hem die pape dede quaet,

. . . .
. . e nichte vanden claghers voerder be
. . wijl ghevangen.
'*Quaet dief*,' sprack hij, 'fel Reynaert
*Dat gh*i mij lief hebt ende waert,
dat hebdi in den lachter mijn
165 *minen ghebode*n ghedaen aenschijn.
*Aen arm man T*ybert ende Brune,
*die noch al b*loedich is sijn crune.
*Ic enwil ni*et vele schelden:
*mer ic denk*e u kele salt ontghelden
170 *noch heden* al op ene wijle.'
'*Nomen pat*er Christe file,'
*sprack R*eynaert, 'here, ende of Brune
noch al bloedich heeft die crune,
heer coninck, wat bes*t*aet mij dat?
175 *Of hi Lantfr*ijts honich at
ende hem die dorper *l*achter dede?
Noch heeft Brune soe starcke lede,
*was hi ghesle*gen of versproken,
*waer hi go*et, hi hadt ghewroken,
180 *eer hi quam* in dat water.
*Efter van T*ybaert die kater,
*dien ic herber*chde ende wel ontfinck,
*ende of hi w*t om stelen ghinck
tot des papen huys, sonder minen raet,
185 *ende hem* die pape dede quaet:

44

'Hir steyt de hane, de heft vorloren
Syn slechte; o, valsche vntruwe deeff!
Dat gy vele seggen, gy hebben my leff,
1725 Dat hebbe gy in deme laster myn,
Vnde is an mynen lûden wol schyn:
Arm man Hyntze vorloß syne sunt
Vnde Brun is noch syn houet vorwunt.
Ik wyl yw nicht vele meer schelden,
1730 Men yuwe hals schal des entgelden.
Hir synt vele klagers vnde schynbar daet;
Dyt alle wyl yw wesen quaet.'
    'Gnedighe here,' sprack Reynke, 'wat schadet
        my datte,
Eft Brunen noch blodich is syne platte?
1735 Wor vmme was he so vormeten
Vnde wolde Rustevylen syn honnich ethen,
Vnde em de bur laster an deden?
Brun is yo so stark van leden!
Is he gheslagen efte vorsproken,
1740 Were he gud, he haddet ghewroken,
Eer he quam in dat water.
Echter ok mede Hyntze de kater,
Den ik herbergede vnde wol entfenck,
Vnde he do vth vmme stelen ghynck
1745 To des papen hus, sunder mynen raet,
Vnde em de pape dede quaet—

bi lode, soudic des ontghelden,
so mochtic mijn gheluc wel schelden.
1855 niet dar bi, her coninc Lioen,
wat ghi wilt, dat moochdi doen
ende ghebieden over mi.
hoe goet, hoe claer mijn sake si,
ghi moocht mi vromen ende schaden.
1860 wildi mi sieden ofte braden
ofte hangen ofte blenden,
ic enmach u niet ontwenden.
wi sijn alle in u bedwanc.
ghi sijt starc ende ic bem cranc.
1865 mijn hulp is clein, die uwe is groot.
twaren, al sloechdi mi doot,
dat ware ene cranke wrake.'
    Recht in deser selver sprake
spranc op Bellijn die ram
1870 ende sijn oei, die mit hem quam,
dat was vrouwe Olewi.
Belijn sprac 'nu toe, ga wi
alle voort mit onser claghen.'
Brune spranc op mit sinen maghen
1875 ende Tibaert sijn gheselle
ende Isegrijn die snelle,
die hase ende dat everswijn:
elc wilde in die claghe sijn.
Panther, die kemel ende Bruneel,
1880 die gans, dat tijtsel ende Lampreel,
Boudwijn die esel, Borreel die stier,

By lode! soude ic des ontghelden
soe mostick mijn gheluc wel schelde
Niet daer by, her coninck Lyon!
wat ghi wilt, dat moechdy doen
190 ende ghebieden over mij.
Hoe goet, hoe claer mijn sake sij,
ghi moecht mij vromen ende scaden.
Wildy mij sieden ofte braden
ofte hangen ofte blenden:
195 ic enmach u niet ontwenden;
wij sijn alle in uwen bedwanck.
Ghi sijt starck ende ic bin cranck.
Mijn hulp is cleyn, die uwe is groot.
Vorwaer, al sloechdi mij doot,
200 dat waer u eene crancke wrake.'
    Recht in deser selver sprake
spranck op Bellijn den ram
ende sijn moeye, die mit hem quam,
dat was dame Olewij.
205 Bellijn sprack: 'Nu toe! gaen wij
alle voert mit onser claghen!'
Brune spranck op mit sinen maghen
ende Tybert sijn gheselle
ende Ysegrim die snelle,
210 die haze ende dat everzwijn:
elck wilde in die claghe sijn.
Panthel, die kemel ende Bruneel,
die gans, dat wezel ende tlampreel
Boudwin den ezel, Borreel den stier,

Seker, scholde ik des entgelden
Vnde ik dar vmme lyden schelden,
Dat were to na yuwer vorstliken kron.
1750 Doch wat gy wylt, dat moghe gy doen
Vnde alzo ghebeden ouer my,
Wo gud vnde klar myne sake ok sy.
Gy mogen my vromen, gy mogen my schaden,
Ja, wyl gy my seden efte braden,
1755 Hangen, koppen efte blenden,
Jo byn ik in yuwer gnaden henden.
Wy synt yo alle in yuwem bedwanck;
Stark sy gy, vnde ik byn kranck,
Myn hulpe is kleyn, de yuwe is groet.
1760 Vorwar, al sloge gy my ok doet,
Dat were yw eyne krancke wrake.
Doch wyl ik al in desser sake
Rechtferdich vnde vprichtich syn.'
     Do sprak rambok, de heet Bellyn:
1765 'Id is recht tyd, wylle wy nu klagen.'
Dar quam Ysegrym myt alle synen magen,
Hyntze de kater vnde Brun de bare
Vnde der deren eyne grote schare;
Lampe de haze vnde de ezel Boldewyn,
1770 Wackerloß de klene, ok de grote hunt Ryn,
Metke de tzeghe vnde Hermen de bock,
Ekeren, weselken, hermelken weren dar ok;
De osse, dat perd, de weren ok dar,
Vele wylder deren eyne grote schar,
1775 Dat herte, dat ree vnde Bokert de beuer,
Kanynen, maerten vnde ok de wylde euer,
Bartolt de adebar vnde Marquart de hegger,
Ok Lûtke de kron was dar alder degger,

47

dat hermel, die wesel waren ooc hier.
Cantecleer ende sine kinder
claechden sere haren hinder
1885 ende maecten groot vederslach.
dat groensel ende Cleenbejach
liep ooc mede in deser schare.
alle dese ghinghen openbare
voor haren here den coninc staen
1890 ende deden den vos Reinaert vaen.

215 dat hermel, die wesel waren oeck hier
Cantecleer ende sijn kinder
claechden seer haren hinder
ende maecten groot vederslach.
Dat troeseel *ende* Cleenbejach
220 liep oeck mede in deser scare.
Alle dese ghinghen openbare
voer haren heere den coninck staen
ende deden den vos Reynaert vaen.

⁋ Hoe die coninck te recht sittet end
gheeft die sentencie, dat men Reynaer
vanghen soude ende bi der kele
hanghen. Dat .xxiiii. capittel.

Tybbeke de and vnde Alheyt de goes:
1780 Desse klageden alle ouer den vos.
Hennynck de hane vnde al syne kynder
Klagheden gantz seer eren hynder.
Noch weren dar der voghele meer
Vnde andere der deren eyn groten heer,
1785 De ik nu nicht al kan nomen;
Desse alle wolden den vos vordomen
Vnde dachten dar vp myt scharpen synnen,
Wo se em syn leuent mochten affwynnen.
Se ghyngen vor den konnynck al;
1790 Dar hordemen klaghe ane tal.

❡ Wo Reynke van velen synen wedderparten
vorklaget wart in swaren saken; wo he yslykem
antwort gaff, doch int leste myt tůghen ouerwunnen
wart vnde to deme dode vorordelt. Dat xx capyttel.

NOTES

PART I

Line

7 *Isengrine* (also l. 10), but l. 37 *Ysegrine*, and l. 209 *Ysegrim*. Reinaert II has *Isegrijn* (l. 1876) and 'Reinke de Vos' (l. 1766) *Ysegrym*. The spelling of the proper names in F. is not consistent. Similarly l. 181 has *Tybaert*, but l. 208 (also l. 166) reads *Tybert*. Reinaert II has *Tibaert*, Reinaert I *Tibeert*, while the name of the tom-cat in 'Reinke de Vos' is *Hyntze* (ll. 1727 and 1742).

17 This line, also l. 43, is half cut away in F. and has been amended after the text of Reinaert II.

51 This line and the following are the subject of the illustration on p. 8. Reinaert carries the capon from the table of the priest [bottom, right-hand corner]. Reinaert drops the capon near to the place where Ysegrim is caught [bottom, left-hand corner]. Ysegrim is unable to get out of the barn as he has grown too fat. Ysegrim is beaten [centre of the picture]. This wood-cut is missing in the Lübeck edition of 'Reinke de Vos.'

73 This line is half cut away in F., amended from Reinaert II.

90 After this line, on page 11, last line but two from the bottom: *daer* is quite clear in the original F., but it has not come out well in the reproduction (p. 10).

91 This line and the following are illustrated on p. 12. They belong to Chapter XXI. The same wood-cut occurs again, much mutilated, on the next leaf of F. Reinaert and the badger are seen in the foreground of the poultry-yard of the nunnery; a church is in the background. Reinaert has just brought his confession to an end, but in spite of his pretended repentance he turns his head towards the chickens for which relapse he is scolded by Grimbaert. This wood-cut served as a model for the illustration occurring in the Low German version of the poem. See Prien's edition, frontispiece.

111 This and the following lines (especially l. 119) occurring in Chapters XXII to XXIV are illustrated by the mutilated wood-cut reproduced on p. 20. On it the fox makes his appearance at the King's court. Reinaert, accompanied by the badger, is seen kneeling humbly on rising ground to the left. A little lower down are seen the wolf, the cock and the tom-cat. Facing the cat only the snout of the bear is still visible, and near the wolf part of the tail of the lion. The unmutilated picture may be seen in the Low German edition of 1498. (Cp. Wolff's edition, p. 137.)

162 Before this line $1\frac{1}{2}$ lines of mutilated gloss are still visible. Of lines 162–85 the first halves are cut away, corresponding to the half page cut away on p. 20. The text has been completed from the reading of Reinaert II.

Page

10 This page has not been reproduced by Culemann in his 'Brokken.' See pp. xx–xxi.

16 Pages 16, 18, 24, 26 are the best preserved pages containing either 29 or 30 lines each.

20 This page and p. 22 represent the worst leaf of F. as half of it has been cut away. The first two lines on p. 22 belong to the much mutilated gloss that probably would have consisted of 5 or 6 lines of which only the last $1\frac{1}{2}$ have been preserved.

26 This page is only half filled because, as a rule, in F. the illustration, occupying a whole page, follows immediately on the title of a new chapter, and there was no room for a full-page wood-cut on p. 26.

PART II

31 Lines 2 and 3 of the Low German gloss seem to have been suggested by lines 46–47 of F.

32 Line 34 in F. is clearly a mistake, the line being repeated from l. 28. The same mistake occurs in 'Reinke de Vos' (l. 1458) which proves the dependence of the Low German poem on the Reinaert Fragments (F.) while Reinaert II (l. 1550) shows the right reading. Reinaert I (l. 1510, Muller's edition) has: Des haddic dicke goet bejach.

38 After l. 1770 Reinaert II has seven lines (ll. 1771–77) that do not occur in F. but are found in 'Reinke de Vos' (ll. 1685–92) where they stand after the heading of Chapter XIX. Chapters XXII and XXIII in F. correspond to Chapter XIX in 'Reinke de Vos.' Chapter XXIV in F. (of which only the title has been preserved) corresponds to Chapter XX in 'Reinke de Vos.' Cp. pp. 48 and 49.

PRINTED
BY

WALTER LEWIS, M.A.

AT THE
CAMBRIDGE
UNIVERSITY
PRESS

For EU product safety concerns, contact us at Calle de José Abascal, 56–1°, 28003 Madrid, Spain or eugpsr@cambridge.org.

www.ingramcontent.com/pod-product-compliance
Ingram Content Group UK Ltd.
Pitfield, Milton Keynes, MK11 3LW, UK
UKHW010049140625
459647UK00012BB/1706